THE
Archive Photographs
SERIES

CHEDDAR

Eve Mills sitting in the back of a minibus with the cubs preparing to leave for the camp at Porlock in the late 1960s. The cubs are David Hewish, Trevor Butcher, Robert Latham, Nigel Appleton, Ian Lewis, -?-, and Patrick Westby. Eve came to live with relatives in Cheddar in 1946 and married her husband Cyril who was billeted in the village following the return of the 1st Suffolk Regiment from Dunkirk. She took over the cub pack in 1952 and retired in 1974. The late Helen Hill was her assistant for many years. Eve's musical ability in writing pantomimes and playing the piano has been a popular feature of village life for some forty years. She was honoured by being a recipient of maundy money in 1993.

THE
Archive Photographs
SERIES

CHEDDAR

Compiled by
Grahame Burnell, Brendon Cottrell, John Gardner, and Fred Villis
on behalf of the Cheddar Valley U3A History Group

CHALFORD

First published 1997
Copyright © Cheddar Valley U3A History Group, 1997

The Chalford Publishing Company
St Mary's Mill, Chalford,
Stroud, Gloucestershire, GL6 8NX

ISBN 0 7524 1048 2

Typesetting and origination by
The Chalford Publishing Company
Printed in Great Britain by
Bailey Print, Dursley, Gloucestershire

Cover picture:
A typical Somerset farmyard scene with the equipment shown in the foreground associated with cider production. The men were obviously persuaded to pose for this picture during a brief rest and smoke. Seated by the dog is a man believed to be Edwin 'Cooper' Thomas who lived in Lower North Street and was responsible for getting the cider barrels ready for the local farmers. He was also a local photographer. Note the man seated on the horse, in the process of rolling a cigarette, paper in mouth.

Contents

The Coat of Arms of Cheddar.

The Cheddar coat of arms is also that of the de Cheddre family. The shield is in two parts: on the left the arms of Sir Thomas de Cheddre, a wool merchant, who died in 1442; on the right the arms of Lady Isabella de Cheddre, who survived her husband by 30 years. Their tombs and monumental brasses are in the chancel of St Andrew's Church. The coat of arms is depicted in at least one of the church's stained-glass windows. The manor-house of the de Cheddres is the present-day Hanam Manor, by the entrance to the Kings of Wessex Community School.

Acknowledgements

Cheddar Valley U3A History Group would like to thank:

All members of the Cheddar Valley U3A History Group who contributed in one way or another to this book; Kevin Wills for prints from the original glass negatives, which form part of his collection; and, also, Mark Bailey for giving us access to his huge collection of Cheddar postcards.

For supplying postcards, photographs, and/or information:

Hugh Alsop, David Beacham, Gillian Bessant, Graham Brewer, Chris and Rita Brice, Harry Broome, Doris Burnell, Marion Burnell, Shirley Cannicott, Jim Carter, John Chinn, Gwen Chiplen, Ethel Day, Pat and Phil Deane, Marjorie Derrick, Roger Durston, Julie Gough, Pat Farrant, George Flinders, Austin Ford, Fred Ford, Pat and John Gardner, Robert Harrill, Marion Heal, Audrey and Tim Hill, Melvyn Hill, Gerald Hopkins, Shirley Hudd (née Adams), Ann and Don Hurford, Gladys Jones, Janet and Roger Keen, Robert and Terry King, John and Betty Lane, Ken Langford, Nick Lewis (of Batts Combe quarry), Bernard Masters, Valerie Maunders, Thelma Maunders, Cecily Millard, Eve Mills, Graham Nicholson, Janet Oatley, Keith Pavey, Eileen Pople, Christine Reynolds, John Scourse, Alan Sealey, Mervyn Sheldon, Jackie Skidmore, Ann Small, Betty Stokes, Nan Thomas, Rex and Nora Thomas, Henry Travis, Hugh Tyson, Eddie Wickham, Mike Woolley, Cheddar First School, Cheddar WI, Cheddar Valley Gazette, and Cheddar Parish Council.

A special thank you to Robert Hill for all his help and encouragement to our group over a long period.

(The cover picture and the pictures on pages 8, 14, 16, 20, 21, 27, 28, 30, 64, 80, 90, and 93 are part of the collection held by Kevin Wills of Axbridge. Copies are available from Kevin.)

Cheddar Gorge in 1913.

Introduction

Cheddar has been inhabited by man since at least the Stone Age. The warm, sheltered climate has made it an ideal place for humans to live. Stone Age remains of human habitation, together with a complete male skeleton were found in the caves in Cheddar Gorge c. 1902. Iron Age man has left signs of occupation and the Romans had a settlement near St Andrew's Church, evidence of which was found during the building of the modern houses in Parsons Pen. There is written evidence in King Alfred's will, dated 901 AD, that there was a royal palace at Cheddar, the outline of which can still be seen in the grounds of the Kings of Wessex School and, following extensive excavation there during the 1960s, much was discovered about Saxon palaces. The remains of the chapel of St Columbanus, which served the palace, can still be seen close by although the stonework left dates from the 13th century and later.

King John gave the manor of Cheddar to Hugh, archdeacon of Wells and it remained in the bishop's hands until 1548 when it passed via Sir Edward Seymour to Sir John Thynne, an ancestor of the present Marquis of Bath. A large part of Cheddar Gorge, including Cheddar Showcaves, is still owned by the marquis.

In the 13th century Henry III granted Cheddar the right to hold a fair and market. Fairs were held on St George's Day (23 April) and St Luke's Day (18 October). The fairs and markets were held on common land in what was Play Street and is now Station Road and there are entries in the parish records in the 17th century concerning expenditure on the various fairs. The Market Cross is a 15th-century preaching cross which a century later had the surrounding arches and a roof added. It has been renovated and restored over the years and is still a favoured meeting place for some of the village folk. The Cross was renovated in 1834 at the expense of the then Lord Bath and High Cross Street, where the Market Cross stands, was renamed Bath Street at this time in his honour.

Looking south from Warrens Hill, c. 1910. The photographer has taken a wide-angle view of the village. In the distance is Nyland Hill and Glastonbury Tor. The chimneys of the paper mill, which were demolished in 1928, can be seen to the left. A careful look reveals many other features built before the turn of the century, when Cheddar's population was less than 2,000.

Kent Street and its old cottages, a group of houses at the entrance to what is now Barrows Croft, the British School and, close by, Hillfields and the railway station, can all be picked out, although you may need the help of a magnifying glass.

Cheddar grew up in two sections, one around the Kings Head public house in Kent Street and another around the church and Market Cross. The road that linked the two became known as Tweentown and still bears that name today.

Cheddar has been famous for its agriculture because of its favoured climate and abundant supply of water. In the latter part of the 19th century strawberry growing was introduced on a commercial basis and at one time the whole village was one large strawberry plantation. Other industries included up to thirteen mills between the caves where the water emerges from underground and the church. These mills dealt mainly with corn and, in later years, paper. Shirt-making was also a prosperous industry at one time, in fact what was to become the Van Heusen shirt company started life at the bottom of the gorge. Then, of course, there is the world-renowned Cheddar cheese. Its origin is a bit vague but there are records of King Henry II in 1170 ordering eighty hundredweight of cheeses to be delivered from Cheddar. An expedition to the Antarctic in 1901 is said to have taken 3,547 pounds of Cheddar cheese from Mr Small's cheese shop in Bath Street.

Cheddar is justifiably proud of its fine church dedicated to St Andrew. It was built mainly in the 14th and 15th centuries, its 110ft high tower being finished in 1421. There are some excellent old windows. The coats of arms of some of Cheddar's old families can be seen including one of the Malherbe family featuring stinging nettles and the motto 'Leave Me Alone'.

Of course, no description of Cheddar would be complete without a mention of its famous gorge and caves. Cox's cave was discovered by accident in 1837 by Mr George Cox who operated the mill where the Cheddar Gorge Hotel (formerly The Cliff Hotel) is now. He needed room to expand his business, so he decided to remove some of the rock opposite and broke into the cave which was full of rich stalactite and stalagmite formations. Gough's cave was opened up by Richard Cox Gough, initially in partnership with Jack and Nancy Beauchamp who lived in a cottage by the cave.

Hannah More, the great pioneer of education on Mendip, opened her first school in Cheddar. The building still exists in Lower North Street and is a favourite meeting place for village activities. The school was financed by a friend of Hannah's, Sir William Wilberforce MP, probably best known for his anti-slavery campaigning. Wilberforce paid a visit to Cheddar and, appalled by the conditions of the inhabitants, he told Hannah More, 'Something must be done for the poor people of Cheddar. If you will be at the trouble, I will be at the expense'. Hannah rented the cottage on a seven-year lease for '6½ guineas a year' and so, on Sunday, 25 October 1789, 140 children gathered at the cottage and were taken to St Andrew's Church for a service. The school opened that day.

Cheddar has been fortunate to have had some of its more recent history well recorded photographically and you will find many aspects of past life in and around the village illustrated in this book. We must thank the photographers, both known and unknown, for this opportunity to see the village as they saw it. We have done our best to be accurate with both names and dates throughout this book. However, as much of the source material was collected from the memories of several villagers, this sometimes resulted in conflicting information. We apologise in advance, therefore, for any errors, hoping that there are no major ones.

One
The Village

The earliest-known written record in which the name of Cheddar appears is in the will of King Alfred. We know from recent archaeological excavations that there was a famous Saxon palace in the field formerly known as 'Yeodens' in Play Street, the road now known as Station Road. The outline of the palace can be seen marked in the grounds of the Kings of Wessex Community School, together with the ruins of the chapel of St Columbanus which was associated with the royal residence. Cheddar's most famous landmark is probably its Market Cross which dates from the 15th century.

This view dating from c. 1910 shows Union Street in the background on the left of the Cross with the Market Cross Hotel to the right. The hotel is still run as a commercial business today.

Bath Street is named after the Marquis of Bath and one of the best-known landmarks in the street is the Bath Arms Hotel. The name dates from *c*. 1830. The original building was known as the George Inn and was the main coaching inn on the Cross to Wells route. This was where Hannah More and her sister stayed when they first came to Cheddar in the late 1780s. In 1902, about the time that this picture was taken, mine host was Mary Timewell who advertised the establishment as a 'Family and Commercial Hotel and Posting House'. The tariff at that time was: room (2/-), breakfast (2/-), luncheon (2/-), dinner (3/6), and tea (1/3). 'Superior Wines and Spirits' and 'Good Stabling and Lockup Coach Houses' were available. In 1936 the old bay-windowed building was bought by Simmonds of Reading, demolished, and the present hotel erected. The building on the left of the picture was used as a storeroom for an auction house. Notice that this building is set back a short distance from the front of the inn. As you walk in front of the Bath Arms today this difference is marked by a kink in the present front-boundary wall.

The building to the left of the Market Cross, was a place of worship known as Christ Church, built by the Budgett family for the 'Reformed Episcopal Church'. The religious organisation that met there was also known as 'The Forward Movement'. This did not last long and the building was then used by the adjacent Brice's shop as a store. When it was demolished, the Regal Cinema was built on the site. In turn, the cinema was converted for a short period to a car showroom for Holders of Congresbury and then later demolished. The site is now occupied by the 'Homestead' flats. The first lady on the right in the doorway of the shop (that is today Deane's) is Mrs Robert Channon, wife of the then shop-owner. In the second doorway is her daughter Gladys Channon (later Thomas), with her younger sister and a friend.

Jacob's Ladder gave this fine view of a rather empty-looking village looking towards Cheddar reservoir, *c.* 1937. The road in the foreground is The Bays and above it is Birch Hill. The corner of the Gardeners Arms in Silver Street can be seen on the extreme right of the picture. On the left, near The Bays, is a building then known as the Chalet Hotel, which still exists but as a private house.

A coach party arrives outside the Bath Arms Hotel, *c.* 1917.

In 1878 George Pedley established his Town and Country Shop in Silver Street. He advertised the departments as: 'Grocery, Provisions, Drapery, Ironmongery, Patent Medicines, Boots and Shoes, Brushes, Fruit, etc.' The specialities were 'Coffee Roasted and Ground Fresh Daily' and 'only Genuine English Cheddar Cheese sold'. Pedley's shop was Cheddar's first 'supermarket' and also sold ready-made clothing and boots. The word 'Pedley' even became part of the local vernacular; apparently the strawberry growers used to buy his boots and when strawberry planting took place the expression 'to pedley the plant' meant firming it into the earth with the boot. The shop was taken over by Edward Giddens in 1914 then sold to Gerald Hopkins in 1948. It closed in 1992 and is now a private residence. This picture dates from about 1910.

Silver Street was originally a main thoroughfare in Cheddar, especially for those visiting the Gorge. The Kings Head Pub, the edge of which can be seen on the left of the picture, dates from the 15th century. In the early 19th century it was called the 'Kings Arms' and is the oldest Cheddar pub still in use with part of it still thatched. During the Second World War, 'S. Durbin' was a fish-and-chip shop and before that it was a butcher's shop. Bill Day who lived in the cottage (centre right) bought soot in bulk from Bristol and sold it for agricultural purposes. He was the son of John Day who in 1910 was the licensee of the Gardeners Arms. The man leaning on his bicycle is postman George Hill on his delivery round.

14

Cheddar's present fire station in The Hayes was built *c.* 1936. The box on the roof was specially constructed by John Scourse to amplify the siren summoning the firemen and during the Second World War it accommodated air-raid sirens. The appliance parked outside is a Leyland fire-engine with a Merryweather pump which came originally from Calne. It was built in the early 1920s. This apparatus was used until the Second World War, when it was replaced by a Humber car and trailer pump.

The road now known as the Lippiatt, shown here *c.* 1900, seems to have had various spellings over the years. The name comes from the Old English for a kind of cattle grid. Domestic cattle could not leap over the obstruction. Most of these cottages still exist.

15

The view from the top of the tower of St Andrew's Church shows the concrete works in Redcliffe Street *c.* 1910. This site was formerly a paper mill started in the 1830s by Tanner Brothers. In 1876 it was trading as Tanner and Budgett; later, in 1890, it was taken over by Wansborough and Warrell and was closed down in 1910. The two chimney stacks were demolished in 1928. There is a stone tablet in the new wall adjacent to Felsberg Way with the Wansborough Paper Company initials – 'WP Co 1898'. This was saved when the site was cleared a few years ago, prior to the building of the houses in Felsberg Way. This large industrial site was used during the First World War (1914-18) for the making of open-back lorries by Burnell Brothers and John Scourse. After the war, production switched to the making of car bodies (about 3,000 a year) for a Birmingham firm. In 1925 Caleb Alrige started the Cheddar Art Potteries on this site. This enterprise closed down in 1968. It is believed that the production of concrete products started on the site in the 1930s. The cottages in the foreground are in Church Street near Church House. The tree-covered area in the centre of the picture is where the Budgens supermarket now stands.

The row of trees in Station Road was planted to mark the diamond jubilee of Queen Victoria in 1897. Hanam Manor is just off the picture to the right near the horse and cart, Ivy Farm is on the left. The picture was taken from a postcard sent in 1904.

This delightful old thatched cottage, in what is now Station Road, was occupied by a coal merchant, George Andrews, until he died in 1947. It was originally called Dare House. James Dare, a former proprietor of the *Weston Mercury*, lived there. Mr Lane built the shop premises which are now known as 'Lanes'. This business traded on the other side of Play Street (now Station Road) from 1923 until it moved to its present site in the early 1950s. The gable end and chimney on the left of the picture are part of the post office.

Miss Annie Phillips (*née* Hill) is by the door with her daughter Margaret on the left, *c.* 1910. The post office in Bath Street has been on this site since about 1860.

Just along from the post office is a shop which for many years traded under the name of 'Channon'. Several generations owned it in succession. Mr Robert Channon was the original owner opening the shop in about 1890. He was followed by his daughter Gladys who started working in the shop when she was 14 years old. She married Stanley Thomas and together they ran the shop and later were joined by their son and his wife, Rex and Nora Thomas. Gladys continued working in the shop until the late 1960s when she was nearly eighty. It was her *life* and she enjoyed it immensely. Rex and Nora retired in 1985. This picture shows the building *c.* 1935. The advertisement on the shop door is for 'Radiac Shirts and Collars' which were made in the shirt factory in the Gorge. The shop premises are still there but the name 'Channon' has gone; it is now called 'Presence'.

18

This shop in Union Street, shown c. 1900, was formerly part of the E.B. Brice buildings and is now Cheddar County Library (since 1976). The stairs in the library which lead up to the exhibition room was the route customers followed to the 'Millinery and Mantles' showroom. Brice's business continued in the next-door premises, Dorchester House, until this became The Wine Shop in July 1997. Four generations of the Brice family ran this business. At one time Brice's shop was across the road where Second Scene now trades and which in the 18th century was the Roebuck Inn. In the early 1930s it was The China Tea Company shop. After that it was Burton's grocer's store. A billhead of the former Brice's store listed them trading as: 'Drapers, Grocers, Ironmongers, Tailors and Outfitters, Funeral Orders executed carefully and promptly. British Wines, Huntley and Palmers Reading Biscuits, Nichols Liquid Annatto [an orange dye], Irish Vells &c., Furniture and W & A Gilbey's wines'. This was a terrific selection of goods for a country store.

Cheddar Hall from the air showing the start of the St Andrews Road development. The picture was taken *c.* 1960 by a local helicopter pilot Bob Smith who had bought the section on the south side of the divided hall.

Weeks's bakery in Cliff Street with Mr Alfred Weeks standing outside. This shop is now the Mayflower Chinese restaurant and take-away.

Mr Crossmith in his Darracq motor-car, c. 1905. He was being driven by Arthur Burnell whose widow Doris still lives at Bleadon near Weston-super-Mare. The vehicle was later used as a taxi to take visitors and local people around the Cheddar area until eventually the owner gave it to his chauffeur. The house in the background, called 'Sungate', is still in Church Street, next to the Market Cross Hotel. Its appearance has hardly changed except for the creeper on the front.

High above the village on the crest of Round House Hill stood the structure that gave the hill its name. Little remains of it now except a low stone wall but in the early part of this century it was let by the Marquis of Bath as a hunting or shooting lodge. The roof was constructed of copper, carefully shaped and joined. There must have been a fearful noise inside during heavy rain. The two ladies are obviously enjoying the sunshine (c. 1905) before their man returns with the 'bag'. Note the two containers in the wicker baskets which almost certainly were used for holding water.

These two strawberry pickers are taking a break from their labours on land above The Bays, c. 1910. These fields belonged to Percy Thomas and Ernest Carter. The rooftop of Cheddar Hall and the Lodge (now the Edelweiss Restaurant) can be seen on the left. The old shirt factory is alongside The Bays pond. The Butchers Arms pub is centre of the picture among the trees and the Chalet Hotel (now a private residence) can just be seen behind a tree. Birch Hill and the entrance to West Lynne are top right.

On the river Yeo near Church Farm, c. 1905. Ernest William Hill, who was the chairman of Cheddar Parish Council from 1946 to 1962, is in the boat at the rear and his father is standing in the front boat on the right. Miss Nell Hill is sitting on the left-hand side of the bridge and Emily Hill is on her right.

Two

Cheddar at Work

Quarrying has taken place on Mendip for thousands of years and Cheddar has had its fair share of this vital industry. Parts of the Gorge were once quarried but today the big quarries are Batts Combe and Callow Rock. Until the mid-1920s Batts Combe was worked by small family businesses, the site being known initially as Small's quarry. Batts Combe quarry as we know it today was founded by Charles Butcher and Frederick Ford in 1926 but, as it grew, its potential was realised by larger companies and, as part of the Amalgamated Roadstone Corporation (ARC), it is now in the Hanson conglomerate. Frederick Ford's sons later founded Chelmscombe quarry on Tuttors Hill.

An aerial view of Batts Combe quarry, c. 1950. Note the still-cultivated plots between the village and the quarry.

Quarry foreman Cliff Winter drills the holes for the charges, prior to blasting at Batts Combe quarry, *c.* 1950.

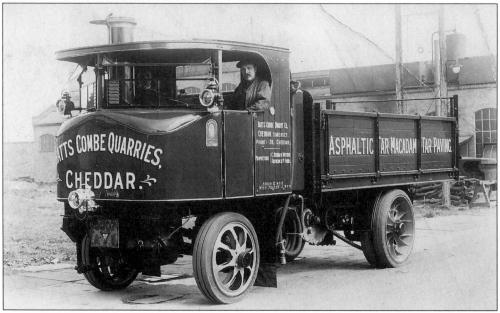

A steam-driven Sentinel lorry owned by Batts Combe quarry, on the site of the old concrete works in Redcliffe Street, *c.* 1920. The barely discernible driver is Charley Savage and his mate is Harold Fountain. The sign-writing on the side of the cab reads: 'Batts Combe Quarry Co. Cheddar, Somerset. Phone 28 Cheddar. Proprietors C. Bernard Butcher, Frederick P. Ford. Speed 12mph, with trailer 5mph'.

160 hundredweight-sacks of lime being loaded onto a trailer drawn by a steam-powered tractor at the limekiln in Callow Rock quarry, *c.* 1925. The average weekly output of lime was approximately 500 tons. The tractor is a Robey (registration number YD 5760) with solid tyres and acetylene lighting. It would haul this eight-ton load to the railway station. Callow Rock quarry on Shipham Hill was founded in 1919 by London bankers Henry and Francis Tiarks, together with J.H. Schroeder, a Swiss banker. This operation is now owned by Camas Aggregates.

Callow Rock quarry delivered some of its products to customers by road using this 1933 Sentinel steam-lorry (YD 9587). Here it is offloading coal transported from Bristol for use in the quarry's gas-production plant *c.* 1937. The driver hand-winding the moving bed of the vehicle is Eddie Flinders – the trailer had to be unloaded by hand. This vehicle, known as *Callow Rock*, is in good working order today and still takes part in traction-engine rallies. Shipham Hill Road can be seen in the background below the quarry.

Burnell Brothers had a cycle and car business in Cheddar in the early 1900s. There were four brothers and a sister: Arthur, Leonard, William, Lawrence, and Flossie. They operated bus and coach services around the locality from the mid-1920s. They also operated a fleet of 30 tractors for a food-production scheme during the First World War and car bodies were made in co-operation with John Scourse the local carpenter. Burnell Brothers were responsible for introducing electric lighting to the village using two 60hp 'National Gas Engines'. The gas was produced on the premises from anthracite. This picture shows Leonard and Arthur Burnell with one of their lorries which had been converted in order to take petrol to Bulford Camp during the First World War.

An important man in the village before the arrival of motor-traffic was the village blacksmith. This smithy in Station Road on the corner of Lower North Street is now an estate agent's office. The man, seen here in the doorway c. 1910, was the then proprietor Mr Gibson. He retired in 1923 and sold the business to Ernest Lane. The shop was the forerunner of Lane's Store which is now opposite. There were three other blacksmiths in Cheddar: Spratt's in Church Street, Frederick Heal's and Harris's. Apparently, it was quite usual for a queue of a dozen horses to be outside the smithy on an icy morning to have 'frost nails' fitted. These were chisel-shaped nails to give the horse a better grip. Another job for this establishment was soldering tins around cheeses that had been sold to tourists in the Gorge and were to be sent overseas as gifts. Every cheese was a different size and so the tins were made individually to fit.

Opposite: The building shown here is still situated at the junction of the Lippiatt and the Gorge, although the façade is somewhat different today. If you look carefully, it is still possible to make out the Burnell name on one end of the building. The vehicles, shown here c. 1920, are four 28-seater Karriers, two 18-seater Napiers, and an AEC with 28 seats. At this period they had solid tyres and a retractable hood made of sail-cloth. The livery of the coaches shown was primrose and black and the name of the fleet was 'Lorna Doone Coaches'. Most of the trips were to Bournemouth, Torquay, Seaton and Weymouth. The charabancs were also used to transport visitors from Cheddar railway station to the Gorge. The fare for this journey was 2d.

There were at least four bakers in Cheddar in the early part of this century. Mr Henry West, seen here with his daughter, delivered bread from his shop in Lower North Street.

Sam Heal's cycle shop was at the corner of The Bays and The Cliffs. During the period between the wars, when radios had to have their accumulators charged regularly, Sam Heal was the man who supplied this service. After the business closed, Eddie Wickham carried on a cycle-repair business.

The postman delivers his mail in all weathers. The horse-drawn mail van, seen here leaving Cocklake post office *c.* 1910, brought the mail to Cheddar and it was then distributed by postmen on foot or by bicycle much as now. The postman (*below right*) is Mr William Hill, seen at the door of 'Jasmine Dene' in Lower North Street.

Strawberries have been a commercial crop in Cheddar since 1901 when Mr Samuel Spencer started growing them. When the crop was ready all the family was pressed into service to harvest them and get them off to market. This medieval cottage, named Gould's Cottage, was in Birch Hill (or Burge Hill as it was known). It was demolished soon after this picture was taken *c*. 1910 and replaced by the present house named 'Gorge View'.

Various methods were used to transport strawberries to the railway station, including handcarts and this two-tiered horse-drawn vehicle. Close inspection will reveal the baskets of strawberries loaded carefully onto the cart.

The Cheddar Valley Railway was opened on the 3 August 1869 as a broad-gauge single line with a distance of 7ft $\frac{1}{4}$ in between the rails. In 1875, in only three days, it was converted to the standard gauge of 4ft $10\frac{1}{2}$ in. It was to provide a link from the main London line at Yatton to the City of Wells. Tourists used the line extensively, with special arrangements made to transport them from the station to the Gorge, and in 1886 there were five passenger trains a day. The Cheddar Valley line also carried milk, stone from the quarries, raw pulp for the paper mills at Wookey and, of course, in the summer, strawberries from Cheddar and the rest of the valley. This trade caused it to be named 'The Strawberry Line'. At Cheddar station the strawberries were loaded on to specially sprung wagons which were designed not to bruise the delicate fruit and were transported all over the country by rail. The large carriages were known as 'Syphon Gs' and the small vans were 'fruit vans'. The picture dates from between the two World Wars.

Staff at Cheddar station in the 1920s. From left to right, front row: Virginia Wilcox (who ran the canteen), Mr Swainson (station-master), and Mr Raines. The back row includes Bert Adams (a shunter), Mr Cottrell, and Mr Welchman.

Mr John Padfield, seen here waiting for the train to come, was one of the signalmen who manned the signal-box in the station-yard at Cheddar. Considerable amounts of stone and lime were transported from Cheddar. There was a special loading ramp west of Five Ways Bridge off Sharpham Road to enable stone from the quarries to be transferred from lorries to railway trucks. The loading platform is still on the side of the Axbridge to Cheddar cycleway.

Coal was a regular cargo carried on the railway to Cheddar and was used by the quarries, the gasworks, the old concrete works, Burnell Brothers (to generate electricity), and, of course, for ordinary domestic consumption. 'A. Perry' was one of several coal-merchants with depots at the station. In this picture dating from *c.* 1920 Alfred Perry is the first man from the left, next are two shunters Mr Welchman and Bert Adams, then the engine-driver and fireman. Mr Perry lived at 'Nyland View', Station Road. His premises and coal-yard were also in Station Road. Coal is still on sale in the vicinity of the old station-yard today, although now it is brought in by road rather than rail.

Cheddar Fire Brigade in about 1930. From left to right, front row: Bert Stickland, Ted Isgar, Ken Benjafield, Vaughan Channon, Ted Hudson, John Sampson, Herb Brooks, and Ernest William Hill; back row: Reg Welchman, Edward Cosh, Henry Hill, Sam Durbin, Stan Brooks, and Vic Filer. This picture was taken at the railway station where the fire-engine was then kept.

A fire-brigade has been an essential part of the village since the parish council voted to spend £60 on fire-fighting equipment on 18 April 1906. After purchasing some very basic equipment, including three builder's ladders and a pair of hand-trucks, the brigade was duly formed in November 1906 and it consisted of one captain, one lieutenant, and ten firemen. The team was called out by someone going to look for them and then, after collecting their equipment, loading it on the hand-cart. They would proceed to the fire pushing the hand-cart.

This building opposite Tweentown Stores is now the ATS tyre depot. It was originally built by Mr A. Simmons for the Salvation Army and later sold to Mr Brice for the Plymouth Brethren after a dispute with their fellows in the hall in Upper North Street. William Gough purchased the property in 1925 and Doug Gough celebrated his 21st birthday there with a grand party. In 1927 it opened as a garage, also offering motor-coach trips. The fare for the Friday return-trip to Bristol was 2s 6d. An all-day trip to the Isle of Wight cost 18/- and London was 10/- return. Petrol was priced at $11\frac{1}{2}d$ per gallon. The building on the left was used as a furniture store in 1910 by William Gough and is now Highnams Dairy.

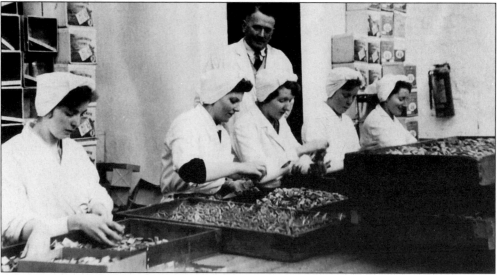

Cheese Straws (Cheddar) Ltd started making their famous cheese straws in the 1930s in the building now occupied by Monkeys Adventure Playground in Tweentown. The recipe used was a carefully guarded secret and the aroma of freshly baked cheese straws around the Tweentown area is still a fond memory. Pictured here are Wilf Harrill, who came to Cheddar as manager just after the Second World War, and, from left to right: Shirley Flinders (later Cambridge), Pearl Flinders (later Young), Janet Keen (*née* Newton), Janet Flinders (later Chiletto), and Anne Green (later Pavey). The factory closed in 1983.

Three
The Churches

Cheddar has its fair share of religious buildings. Ranging from the oldest, the parish church of St Andrew, to the newest, the Roman Catholic Church in Tweentown, they also include buildings for the Methodists, the Baptists, and several other smaller establishments.

Inside St Andrew's Church where the chancel arch was decorated with tiles in Victorian times. The picture shows the church as it was before the First World War. Since then the decorative panels around the chancel arch and next to the altar have been painted over. The oak panelling in the choir stalls and priests' stalls remains as does the finely carved stone pulpit, which dates from about 1450.

A group of bell ringers outside the vestry door of St Andrew's Church, *c.* 1900. In 1885 the ringers of St Andrew's were George Pavey (captain), Thomas Isgar, Albert Gilling, John Coles, William Hill, George Hill, Edward Hill, George Withers, and George Salvage but it is not known if any of these appear in this picture. The men were required to ring the six bells on the first Sunday of the month from 7am to 8am, at Christmas, New Year, Easter Day, Whit Sunday, and Harvest Festival and, in addition, at 'weddings and occasions of rejoicing and mourning'. Practice was only during the winter months.

St Andrew's Church from the south side in 1912, with an excellent view of the fine tower which houses the peal of bells. St Andrew's Church is mainly a 14th- and 15th-century building. Its tower is 110ft high and each year, on Ascension Day, pupils from nearby schools still climb the tower and, after a short service, sing the hymn *Hail the day that sees Him rise*. This was a custom in Oxford colleges and in Cheddar it dates from 1883 when the then vicar of Cheddar introduced it for pupils of the National School.

The Baptist Chapel in Lower North Street was opened on Tuesday, 18 October 1831. This picture is dated pre-1875 because in that year it was decided to put slates on the roof during a building restoration. The records show that for a two-year period from 1847 to 1849 the chapel was without a pastor and a number of members and an assistant preacher emigrated to America or Australia. In 1880 William Clark JP gave a freehold site in the Barrows to build a house for the minister at a cost of £553.

NEW
Baptist Chapel, Cheddar.

On TUESDAY, Oct. 18, 1831,

THE ABOVE CHAPEL WILL BE

OPENED

For Divine Worship,

WHEN TWO

SERMONS

WILL BE PREACHED ON THE OCCASION.

IN THE MORNING,

By the Rev. THOMAS GROSER,

OF WELLS,

Service to commence at Eleven o'Clock.

AND IN THE EVENING,

By the Rev. THOMAS WINTER,

OF BRISTOL,

Service to commence at Half-past Five o'Clock.

There will be a Collection after each Service towards Defraying the Expenses of the Building.

Printed by J. G. FULLER, St. Stephen's Avenue, Bristol.

The Methodist Church premises in Cheddar date from 1820. The present building in Cliff Street was completed in 1897 and is the third Methodist building to stand in the Cheddar area. It was financed by Sidney Hill of Langford House and is one of five of similar design to be built in the Cheddar Valley. The construction of the building was undertaken by Isaac Ford, a local builder, with John Scourse and John Cole undertaking the woodwork and plumbing. The architects were Foster and Woods of Bristol. This postcard dates from *c.* 1905.

The laying of the foundation stone for Our Lady of the Apostles Catholic Church in Tweentown, May 1965. This church was completed in 1966 and is the most modern of Cheddar's religious buildings. It is on the site of an old farmhouse owned by Mrs Mary O'Donnell, a member of the church. On the left is Father Hayes who came to Cheddar in 1959 and served the church for 21 years. Before the present church was built, mass took take place in nearby Pavey's Lane in Acacia House (now known as Old Chapel Cottage) which was purchased in 1942. However, the first place for Catholic worship in the area was a wooden hut provided by the builders of Cheddar reservoir in the early 1930s for use by their many Irish labourers. It was sited at the reservoir.

Four
Cheddar People

In any record of Cheddar, be it a directory or memorial, the same names appear regularly. In recent years Cheddar, like many other Somerset villages, has grown and a good number of people have moved into the area to swell the population. However, names like Pavey, Gough, Starr, King, White, Durston, Alsop, Brice, Heal, Ford, Hill, Scourse, Small, and Thomas, to name just a few, appear regularly. A visit to the war memorial or churchyard will remind one of many of these who have played their part in village life, frequently being prominent in the organisation of village activities and work.

Probably the best-known name in Cheddar is that of Richard Cox Gough (1827-1902). He was a retired sea captain who came to live in Cheddar about 1870, and became fascinated by the caves. He soon entered into partnership with Jack and Nancy Beauchamp who lived in a cottage by the caves and showed visitors around. Gough was responsible for excavating and extending the caves and installing gas lighting, to be followed later by electric lighting. He had eleven children: William, Arthur, Edward, Amy, Llewelyn, Louise, Minnie, Eliza, Thomas, James, and Sarah. With one of his brothers, William discovered the skeleton of a prehistoric man in Gough's Cave. Recent tests, which provoked widespread media interest, found a school-teacher living in the village who has DNA links with these bones.

Douglas ('Doug') Gough (son of William and Minnie Gough) is seen here below a painting of his grandfather, Richard Cox Gough. Although Doug helped in the caves during the school holidays, his main love was engines and motor-cars. He served an apprenticeship at the Bristol Tramways and Carriage Company and started his own garage business in 1927. He also founded Cheddar Veteran and Vintage Car Museum in the Gorge in 1964 and was a director of Burnell Motors 1947 Ltd, which eventually became part of Gough's (Cheddar) Ltd. He died in 1991.

Doug Gough in his 'Nimble 9' with John Lane as passenger in the early '50s. A number of vintage vehicles were restored by Doug Gough including *Caroline*, a 1913 Enfield 'Nimble 9' car which he drove through Belgium and Holland in 1957 and 1958.

Members of the Gough family are seen here *c.* 1900 at the home of Richard Cox Gough, Lion Rock House. He is third from the left and the others are, from left to right: his son Edward, his wife Frances (*née* Jones Powell), his daughter Amy, and his sons Llewelyn and Arthur.

Betsy Card (sitting) was a well-known Cheddar character at the turn of the century. She lived in the Gorge and would sit outside her cottage selling bits of stone and spar to visitors. This picture is on a postcard addressed to 'Mrs L. King, Holly House, The Cliffs' and is signed 'from Betsy'.

This family snapshot is of the Hudson family (Janet Oatley's ancestors) in the 1890s. Janet still lives in the village with her husband David. Her great-grandfather William Hudson (with the beard) was a local baker and he is seen here with his nine children. Janet's grandmother Octavia is the little girl on her father's knee (third from left). The three other younger girls, from left to right, are Bessie, Nellie and Emily.

Left: John Scourse (seen here aged about 90, *c.* 1865) was the great-grandfather of the John Scourse who still lives in the village. He is shown seated with the Hill brothers, George (born 1858) and Edward (born 1861), who lived at the post office. The picture was taken where Lloyds Bank's cash-point can now be found. *Right*: James Rogers and his wife Sarah (*née* Hill), outside their home, Church House Farm. James died in 1917. The arched doorway and the old farmhouse in the background can still be seen today. Church House farmhouse dates back to the 17th century. There is a parish record which lists the half-year's rent at that time as 2/2.

Left: Tom King and his sister Eliza (later Weeks) with their mother and father, Mr and Mrs William King, *c*. 1890. William King, who lived at Sycamore House in the Gorge, was listed as a lime-burner in 1897 and was also involved with the tourist trade in the Gorge. *Right*: in 1899 Tom King was captain of Cheddar cricket team and he is seen here as a young man on the left of the picture, together with Eddie Gough (standing) and two friends. Tom King is described as a market gardener both in 1897 and in 1910. He lived at Holly House in the Gorge.

Lt Colonel Edward Hyde Openshaw and his son Edward Reginald (known as 'Copper'), *c*. 1900, in the garden of their home 'Burrough House', in what is now Barrows Croft. Both served their country: Lt Colonel Openshaw was a doctor in partnership with Dr Statham (as surgeon) and was second-in-command of the 1st/4th Somersets in the First World War, dying in Mesopotamia. 'Copper', who had his own small plane, was in the Royal Flying Corps in the First World War and was a group captain in the RAF in the second. 'Copper' had a landing strip near his house in Cheddar and there is a story about him flying in at one end of Cheddar station and out the other. Copper Close in Cheddar perpetuates his name.

The children of Mr Robert Channon posing with a friendly looking horse, *c*. 1900. From left to right: Percy, Elsie, and Gladys Channon. Mr Channon kept the ladies and gentlemen's outfitter's shop in Bath Street from 1890. He was followed by his daughter Gladys and then by her son Rex Thomas, who carried on the business with his wife Nora until 1985.

Margery Hicks is on the left of this picture taken in the early years of this century with her mother Eliza Heal (right) outside what is now 'The Galleries' in the Gorge. Margery and her mother lived there for many years until they moved to Bays Cottage after the First World War. Margery was the grandmother of Melvyn Hill, who supplied a number of photographs and postcards used in this book.

Alfred and John Scourse in the 1930s in the timber-yard associated with their woodworking factory which was where Lloyds Bank car park and Punnet Close are now sited. In the background are imported logs of Russian aspen which were used to make the strawberry baskets. There is a large black poplar tree, which is now the subject of a preservation order, in the garden of a house in Punnet Close. It grew from a cutting from a log in the timber-yard.

The Hembury family in their strawberry field in Lower North Street, c. 1920. Tweentown is in the background; the ivy-covered gable-end on the right is the rear of the 'Lanier' company building; to the right and behind this is the site of Cheddar Cheese Straws Factory, now Monkeys Adventure Playground. The boy in the centre is Felix Hembury, his father John is on the left, his brother Jack is third from left, and his mother is third from the right.

A Lewis/Scourse family group photographed during November 1914 behind the Valley Hotel in Union Street. The hotel is now a private house which backs on to the rear of the health centre. John Scourse's maternal grandfather was William Day Lewis who married Eliza Jane Swearse and owned the Valley Hotel in Union Street. He was a founder member of Cheddar Parish Council and was also a member of Axbridge Rural District Council for many years. His cousin was Captain Arthur Lewis who married William Day's sister Emma. John's paternal grandfather was also named John Scourse. He succeeded to the building and undertaking business which was continued by his son Alfred and Alfred's son, the present John Scourse. From left to right, back row: -?-, Captain Arthur Lewis, Granny Lewis, a soldier, Daisy Scourse with baby Nancy, Fred Scourse with daughter Joan, Lilias Lewis with daughter Winifred, a soldier, William Day ('Grandpa') Lewis, Peg Scourse, Dick Lewis, Garnet Lewis and Rosa Stocker (later his wife), a soldier, Bertha Lewis (wife of Dick and the daughter of William Chatterton-Dix, who composed the epiphany hymn *As with gladness, men of old*), Dorothy ('Dolly') Stubbings, Emma Lewis (wife of Arthur), Edgar Stubbings, William Lewis Jnr, Isabella Robson and A.E. Robson. The children with the rope are from left to right: -?-, Biddy Stubbings (later Willans), -?-, Mary Lewis, Barbara Lewis (later McKenzie), Julie Lewis, Betty Scourse (later Howard), Nancy Lewis, Dorothy Scourse (later Glanville), and William Lewis.

Dr R.W. Statham on his motor-cycle and his wife Nessie in their car, c. 1908. Reginald Whiteside Statham lived at The Hall, in what is now St Andrews Road, from 1892, when he purchased it, until he died in 1934. Dr Statham had his surgery there for many years and he was also deputy coroner for Somerset and, for some fifty years, a churchwarden of St Andrew's. After his death, his widow continued to live at The Hall until she died in 1945. Dr Statham MRCS Eng, LSA, JP was also surgeon and medical officer for Axbridge District No 8, public vaccinator, certifying factory surgeon and medical attendant at St Michael's Home for 'consumptive patients of both sexes'. He helped bring up many of the poor people in Cheddar by giving them what they needed, including milk from his own cows free from tuberculosis.

The house known as The Hall is thought to have been built in the 16th century on the site of an earlier manor-house. It has been added to over the years and was sold following the death of Mrs Statham in 1945. Some fifteen years later it was converted into four separate dwellings. The estate agent's sale document (a copy of which still exists) described The Hall as 'an interesting Tudor/Queen Anne Manor House. Skilfully modernised, amidst beautifully timbered and secluded grounds with entrance lodge, outbuildings and pasture land. The whole extending to a little under nine acres. Natural Parkland bounded by The Cheddar Water which issues from the Gorge'. The lodge is now the Edelweiss restaurant, and the St Andrews Road development was built on the grounds of The Hall in the early 1960s.

A school outing to the Cliff Hotel tea gardens in the 1880s. The stone grotto in the background is now incorporated into Gill and Malcolm Scard's crazy-golf course. The only person that it has been possible to identify is Eliza Jane Swearse (*née* Lewis) who is fifth from the left in the front row.

These card players pictured *c.* 1900 at the rear of the Valley Hotel in Union Street include Frederick W. Brooks, a founder member of Cheddar Parish Council (left), James Brice, who farmed in Kent Street (centre), and, on the right, Mr Branch and William Day Lewis, the latter being chairman of the parish council from 1896 until 1900.

From left to right in the back row of this picture, dated *c*. 1945, are Lionel Durston, who farmed at Church Farm; Kenneth Toms, who worked abroad for a large part of his working life; and Frank White who worked in a solicitor's office in Wells. In the second row are Lionel's wife Eveline (*née* King); Lilian King, the daughter of James and Sarah Rogers of Church Farm House (*see page 42*); Dinah Toms (*née* King), wife of Kenneth; and Nina White (*née* King), wife of Frank. The children in the front row are: Roger Durston, who succeeded his father Lionel at Church Farm; Roger's sister Jean Webber (*née* Robertson); and Jackie Skidmore (*née* White) who is still a popular member of the library staff today.

Left: Eveline King at the doorway of her hairdresser's shop in Cliff Street *c*. 1930. She later married Lionel Durston of Church Farm. The shop-front is now part of a private dwelling called 'Roseneath'. *Right*: Bill Gould who kept Cheddar clean and tidy for some forty years from about 1910 to 1950. The picture was taken *c*. 1942.

The Regal Cinema, at the junction of Union Street and Church Street, was one of the last cinemas built in England before the Second World War. It opened on 18 September 1939 at 5.30pm. Its first programme, showing on Monday, Tuesday and Wednesday, was Leslie Howard and Wendy Hillier in *Pygmalion* with Mickey Mouse in colour as a supporting feature. Later in the week Errol Flynn and Olivia de Havilland starred in *The Adventures of Robin Hood*. The business was owned at one time by Regal Cinema (Cheddar) Ltd, whose directors included Clarence Reeves, George Gilling, and Hubert Pimm. In 1952 the *Kinematograph Year Book* stated it had '400 seats, a Western Electric Sound System, with films delivered by Film Transport Service'. The films were stated to be 'continuous Monday to Friday from 5pm and on Saturdays at 2pm, 5pm and 7.45pm'. With the increase in the popularity of television having an adverse effect on attendances, the cinema closed about 1958.

Edgar Day was the projectionist at Cheddar's Regal Cinema from 1946 until it closed. Edgar worked at one of the quarries and his working day was arranged so that he left in time to project the first films at 5pm at the cinema. His wife Ethel was one of the cinema's first usherettes. Edgar was also a well-known drummer and often played the drums at local functions.

Five

Growing Up in Cheddar

When William Wilberforce MP visited Cheddar in 1789 at the suggestion of Hannah More, he was appalled by the conditions in which people lived. On returning to Hannah More's house at Wrington he said, 'Miss More, something must be done for the poor people of Cheddar'. He offered to finance a school if Hannah More, who was an experienced school-teacher, would organise it. On 25 October 1789 140 children gathered at what is now known as 'Hannah More Cottage' to inaugurate her Sunday school. The building was originally a cottage with an ox barn attached. In 1789 it was given a new thatched roof and some additional windows. The building still stands in Lower North Street.

'Hannah More Cottage' was purchased by the parish council in 1953 and is today used by various community groups as a meeting place.

When Hannah More died in 1833 she left the sum of £50 towards the cost of a new school in Cheddar. The Marquis of Bath gave £100 and the remainder was raised by public subscription. The National School opened in Lower North Street in 1836 (the date on the postcard is incorrect!). The school mainly took pupils who were Church of England. Mr W. Woodgate was headmaster in the 1940s, followed by Ivor Williams. It closed in 1964 when the Kings of Wessex School opened. The building was then occupied for several years by Fountain Forestry. It has now been converted into flats called Hannah More Court, right next-door to the original 'Hannah More Cottage'.

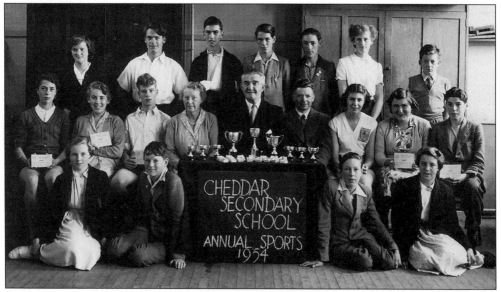

Pupils from the Cheddar Secondary School (formerly the National School) at their annual sports prize-giving day in 1954. From left to right, back row: Margaret Harrill, Paul Rodda, John Miller, Tony Symons, Colin Maunders, Margaret Smith, and Tony Packer; middle row: Jenny Hale, -?-, Andy Ford, Mrs Honeysett, Ivor Williams (headmaster), Mr Davis, Carol Gould, Pam Lane, and Edward Pavey; front row: Ann Woolley, Peter Bridge, Michael Frances, and Wendy Oatley.

In March 1866 Miss Amy Jordan (later Mrs Jefferies) took the headship of the British School which is now Cheddar First School in The Hayes. She continued with only a short break until 12 November 1909. She was apparently an outstanding head and the school and its children were the centre of her life. The British School started life in two cottages in Union Street in 1845. The first two teachers were Miss Collard and Miss Olive Venn. Pupils paid one penny per week to attend at this time. The school transferred to the Baptist Chapel from 1866 until 1872 and the present school building was opened on 2 January 1872 with accommodation for 130 children. At that time a mistress's salary was £35 1s 10d per annum and an assistant earned £4. The school was enlarged in the late 19th century and in 1901 the Marquis of Bath gave some land which is now the school's playing field.

Mr Edward Walter Pope (centre), headmaster of the Interdenominational (known as the British) School from 1909 to 1921. The British School and its successors has only had nine headteachers in over 150 years. Amy Jefferies was succeeded by Edward Pope in 1909 and John Tyson took over in 1921. He served the school for 35 years before retiring in 1956. His other main interest was scouting and he was still involved in this even in his 80s. John Tyson was followed as head by John Tindsley (1956-60), Robert Birch (1960-67), and Don Higginbottom (1968-88). The present head is Mrs Ilona Bellion. The school was called the British School until 1902, the Interdenominational School until 1935, the Council Junior School until 1945, and, thereafter, the County Primary School. The first name stuck, however, and the school continued to be known locally as 'the British'.

A class at the 'British' School, *c.* 1925. From right to left, back row: H. Brooks, A. Stapleton, D. Ham, G. Flinders, E. Brooks, G. Ham, L. Woolley; second row: Marion Ham, Myrtle Small, Ivy Thomas, Doris Williams, Eileen Lovell, Lillian Carter, Gwen Pavey, Beryl Gough; third row: Joan Thomas, ? Jefferies, Elsie Isgar, Hetty Maine, Mary Scourse, Nina King, Hilda Davis, Clifford Thomas, front row: Nellie Pavey, Edward Cosh, Eileen Reynolds, Bert Reynolds, Winnie Giddings, Eileen Thomas.

A class from the 'British' School, 1939. From left to right, standing: Gerald Hale, Brian Hillier, Beryl Hooper, Joyce Stone, John Chinn, Mary Liddiard; middle row: John Brooks, Dennis Reeves, Richard Brown, Herbert Cullen, Joyce Barber, June Adams, Michael Hardwich, Vilma Stevens, Victor Moulton; front row: William Frost, Fay Hodges, Ellen Reed, Leonard Flinders, Betty Bacon.

Cheddar children, c. 1915, being given a lift to school or maybe to the station for a train ride to school in Wells. Standing are Irene Thomas (left) and Ethel Thomas.

Cheddar Primary School recorder band from the music class of 1956. The band competed successfully at the Bath Festival. From left to right, back row: Joy Heal, Sheila Hamilton, Patricia Ham, Lyn Thomas, Josephine Ford, Dawn Hawkins, Janet Parker, Fiona Beadle, Rosemary Tashimowitz, Margaret Hooper, Pat Butcher, Valerie Skinner; middle row: Helen Boswell, -?-, Penny Hewlett, Sally Pavey, John Tindsley (headmaster), Mr Price (music teacher), Alison Hunt, Sue Parker, Sarah Edwards, Valerie Harris; front row: Sally Dene, Carol Oakley, Maurice Day, Gregory Villis, Bernard Young, Roger Hooper, Graham Alsop, Grenville May, Jennifer Chew.

This happy crowd is thought to be off on a charabanc trip to London, sometime in 1933. Among those on the outing were Alan Jennings, Dudley Davies, Terry King (*née* Heal), Eileen Pople (*née* Starr), Hugh Tyson, Audrey Ford, Betty Lane, Billy Cross, Ron Leigh, Mrs Tyson, Mrs Heal, Cora Ham, Nellie Frost, Joan Pope, Dorothy Ford, Alf Sheldon, Peter Saye, Roy Fountain, Mrs Spencer, Mrs Ham, Mrs Chew, Stan Stubbs, Les Hewlett, Clar Adams, Mrs Pope, Mrs Thomas, John Tyson, Queenie Small, Roy Jennings, and Vernon Leigh.

Cheddar boys getting a lift up The Hayes from the station after attending the Blue School in Wells in the 1930s. The boy holding the reins is Hugh Tyson, son of the 'British' School headmaster John Tyson. The man standing in the cart is Charlie Jennings.

This elegantly dressed young man is said to have cycled from Cheddar to Sexey's School every day on his penny-farthing. Unfortunately, his name is not known. You may wonder how elegant he looked if it was raining; imagine the water and mud being thrown off that large front wheel! The original location of Sexey's School was at Cedar Tree House at Stoughton. It moved to Blackford in 1899.

The Girls Friendly Society of Cheddar dressed up to perform a play called *Queen of the Roses* in the grounds of Cheddar Hall, *c.* 1909. Back row, men: Mr Futcher and J. Hembury; ladies: M. King, J. Bisgrove (later Small), M. Durston (later Whiting), S. Williams (later Banbury), and E. Heal (later Hembury). Middle row: M. Heal (later Hicks), N. Hill (later Portas), F. Isgar, M. Perry (later Isgar), G. Heal (later Fisher), J. Raines, B. Hill, K. Durston (later Andrews), G. Gilling (later Simmons). Front row: F. Raines, N. Hyatt, F. Starr, M. Durston (later Stoneman), F. King (later Bailey).

Cheddar Girl Guides, *c.* 1922. From left to right, top row: Dorothy Scourse, Nancy Lewis, Florrie Schofield, Margaret Scourse, Ida Gough, Eveline King, Betty Scourse; middle row: Jessica Gough, Beryl Gough, Jane Pavey, Eileen Lovell, Gwen Weeks, Nina King; front row: Marion Gough, Doris Jefferies, Lillian Carter, Mabel Benjafield, Marion Carter. Cheddar Girl Guides were formed in the early 1920s by Mrs Schofield, the wife of the Methodist minister. They moved to their present headquarters in The Hayes in 1955. Previously, they met in Dr Kemm's house 'Sunnyside' in Lower North Street (now 'The Dolphins'), and Mrs Kemm was then guide leader. She was followed by Mrs Morrissey, and then by Audrey Hill, who was guide leader for many years.

Some of Cheddar Brownie Pack *c.* 1922 posing beautifully in front of Mrs Kitty Schroeder are (from left): Gwyneth Scourse, Nancy Scourse, Cicely Schroeder, Stella Spratt, and Marion Spratt. Straw hats were part of the all-brown uniform for brownies at this time with their emblem a little gnome. The girls are outside 'Jasmine Dene' in Lower North Street. The brownies in Cheddar started soon after the guides with Mrs Schroeder as brown owl. Her daughter, now Mrs Cicely Millard, was one of the village's first brownies.

Cheddar Girl Guides in 1956. From left to right, back row: Susan Dean, Pamela Cooper, Wendy Bagwell, Lorraine Pavey, Jennifer Parsons, Carol Ford, Fiona Beadle, Rosemary Alway, Marie Parker; second row: Janet Parker, Tessa Senior, Diane Padfield, Jackie Hill, Margaret Reynolds, Ann Hamilton, Elaine Hamilton; third row: Jackie White, Miss Tuffin, Mrs D. Morrissey, Mrs K. Kemm, Mrs A. Hill, Frances Tyler, Cynthia Ham; front row: -?-, Jennifer Payne, Pauline Thompson, Vera and Valerie Moulton, Valerie Day.

Scouting in Cheddar probably started around 1909, although there are no records from this time. The picture shows the 1st Cheddar Scouts in 1921. On the right is Mr J.J. Tyson who was headmaster at the 'British' School. He had succeeded Rev Schofield, who ran scouts in the Methodist Church Hall. Darrell Robertson 'restarted' Cheddar Scouts in 1929 when eight boys met in a local farmer's hayloft. One of the boys concerned was Les Scamp whose mother was also scout-mistress for several years during the Second World War. It was quite unusual to have a lady scouter in those days.

At scout camp in the 1930s. The scouts at the rear are Douglas Heal and Les Scamp and in front are Ron Derrick, Ron Durbin, and Gerald Hopkins. The Cheddar troop continued during the Second World War but it was not until 1954 that it had its own headquarters, when an ex-Army hut was erected at Cheddar First School at a cost of £70. Cubs and scouts met there until 1965 when another wooden hut was erected on land at the top of Lower North Street. This site was sold in 1980 and provided enough money, together with other fund-raising events, to build the present headquarters on land again at Cheddar First School.

A building at the back of St Andrew's Vicarage was the home of scouting during the Second World War. Together with several evacuees who had joined scouts, they formed a band and kept going despite the absence of an adult leader. The troop is pictured here in 1942. From left to right, back row: Eddie Galvin, John Attwood, Cecil Law, Michael Williams, Eric Wooldridge (evacuee); middle row: Robin Reeves, Richard Manthorpe (evacuee), Philip Robbins, Wilf Chinn; front row: Eric Barber, Richard Brown, Raymond Young, John Chinn, Bert Gould.

St Andrew's Church Bible class at the Sugar Loaf in the Gorge, c. 1928. From left to right, front row: Gerald Hopkins, Dennis Welchman, Percy Barrett, and Reg Fulbrook. Among the boys in the back row: ? Reynolds, Russell Robertson, and Arnold Hill (on the right).

The characters in this play at the Methodist Church in Cliff Street *c*. 1925 were, from left to right, at rear: George Ham and George Flinders; in front: Bessie Harris, Clifford Thomas, Nina White (all in white), and Ronnie Greenstock.

The Bishop of Taunton, the Rt Rev Francis West, officially opened the Kings of Wessex Church of England Secondary School in October 1965. Harry Broome (fifth from the right) was the first headmaster, leaving in 1976 to become head of Fairlands, the new middle school. Rev (later Prebendary) Ronald Denman, vicar of Cheddar, is far left, and John Tyson is the fourth from the right; third right is Mrs Nancy Greenhill JP, and sixth right is Dr Rupert St John Kemm. The school stands on the site of a former Saxon palace and the new building was re-sited in order to display the layout of the palace at the front of the building. It became a comprehensive school in 1976 when Keith Herring was appointed headmaster.

Six

Special Events

Cheddar people were very fond of celebrating both national and local events by dressing up and having a procession round the village and, no doubt, some sort of party afterwards. Photographs were taken of these processions but sometimes it has proved difficult to identify exactly which event is being celebrated. The route always seemed to include Bath Street and Tweentown, this being a convenient circular route around the main part of the village.

Queen Victoria's diamond jubilee procession outside the suitably decorated Bath Arms, Bath Street, 1897. A point of interest in this picture is the small bell-tower on the top of the chapel building at the end of the street. In later pictures (*see page 12*) this structure has disappeared.

A procession to celebrate the coronation of King George V on 22 June 1911. The parade is just approaching the top of Lower North Street, an area known as Sergeants Corner. The Catholic Church is now sited just off the picture to the right.

This procession to celebrate the coronation of King Edward VII in 1902 is passing Mr William Small's 'Genuine Cheddar Cheese Store' in Bath Street. In recent years this has been the site of a Gateway store and is currently run by Rupert and Liz Morris under the 'Spar' facia. It has also been a butcher's shop in its time. Farther down the street, on the left, the frontage of the old Bath Arms can be seen and the building on the extreme right is the post office.

During the Boer War in South Africa, Mafeking was under siege from 12 October 1899 until 17 May 1900. Cheddar celebrated the relief of Mafeking with a procession and thanksgiving service on Wednesday, 27 June 1900. The carriage is thought to have been brought to pose outside the photographer's premises in Bath Street. The small boy on the pony is 'Copper' Openshaw, and the man on the horse is Rex Thomas's grandfather, Robert Channon (former proprietor of Channon's shop in Bath Street). The boy holding the horse is Percy Channon, son of Robert. A series of plates was also produced to commemorate the occasion.

Cheddar is blessed with plentiful supplies of water but at times it has too much. Flooding has been a constant problem. In 1904 the river Yeo, which emerges close to Gough's Cave, flooded the fields between the football ground and Hythe Bow. The water was deep enough to allow boating in the fields. The young men are clearly enjoying the occasion although whether the local farmer did is not so certain.

In August 1930 large amounts of water emerged from Gough's Cave causing considerable damage in the Gorge. The caves are natural watercourses and so it can be expected that during periods of heavy rain the water level can rise quite quickly in the subterranean passages which normally are below the level of the showcaves. Occasionally, under adverse conditions, the worst happens as our pictures here and on the next page show.

During the evening of Wednesday, 10 July 1968, a series of very severe thunderstorms passed over the Mendip Hills and six inches of rain in a 24-hour period were recorded by the river authorities on some of the higher parts of Mendip. This resulted in serious flooding in Cheddar Gorge and parts of the village causing considerable damage. The road surface in a large part of the Gorge had to be remade and numerous houses and bungalows close to the river suffered quite severe flooding. Once again, a large volume of water came flooding out of Cheddar Showcaves. The white Vauxhall car belonged to Gerald Robertson, the showcave's manager. Mr Robertson was killed in the air disaster when over a hundred people from the Axbridge and Cheddar area died on a charter flight which crashed in Switzerland on 10 April 1973.

This Austin A35 car was photographed at the time of the 1968 floods in the vicinity of the present tourist information centre. The wall on the right still exists on the edge of the lake opposite Holly House in the Gorge.

In June 1939 Queen Mary (the widow of King George V) visited Cheddar Showcaves. It is presumed that it was a private visit as there appear to be no records in the local press and there is not a very big crowd present. King George VI also visited Cheddar on 2 April 1941 and a brass plate in the present Bath Arms Hotel commemorates the occasion.

What is believed to have been the first motor accident in Cheddar occurred c. 1910. Burnell Brothers' 14-seater charabanc, which was used as a local taxi, collided with another car at the junction of Redcliffe Street, Cliff Street, and Union Street, an area then known as 'Coles Corner'. The building on the left with the tiled roof has of recent years been known as 'Dorothy's', but is now 'Gentle Tone'.

Cheddar Fire Brigade and helpers pose for the camera after building the jubilee beacon on Nyland Hill to celebrate the silver jubilee of King George V on 6 May 1935. The three firemen on top of the pile are, from left to right: Henry Hill, Sam Durbin, and (not in uniform) Melvyn Hill's father Arnold. In the middle row the fireman is Victor Filer, and to the right are Reg Gould and (without a coat) Wilfred Hill (who was clerk to the parish council from 1922 to 1962). In the bottom row, the first man on the left is Mr Young, then Mr Willmott; the fireman in the centre is Laurie Hill, then George Hill, and the fireman on the right is Edward Isgar.

The church fête held at Cheddar Hall, in what is now St Andrews Road, c. 1900. On the left, in front of the seat is the bearded Prebendary F. Clarke (the vicar of Cheddar from 1896 to 1910). Next to him the young boy is 'Copper' Openshaw and then Miss Clarke, the vicar's sister. The man in the white suit is Dr Reginald Statham, the owner of Cheddar Hall.

The tradition of dressing up and having a procession continues in Cheddar. This picture was taken c. 1950 on the occasion of the Cheddar Fête. The boy in the hopper is Austin Ford and he is with his father George Ford and George Pavey while at the rear is Austin's sister Christine. The vehicle is a Chaseside Mechanical Shovel and it is followed by a Bedford lorry. The picture was taken at what was then known as 'Coles Corner' (see page 68).

These ladies, and one young man, are dressed up for the garden fête held to celebrate the Festival of Britain in 1951. The picture was taken at Froglands Farm where the fêtes were frequently held. The lady second from the left is Marion Ham. Also in the picture are Pat Askam and Cynthia Ham. The young man is thought to be Dr Ward's son.

Henry Hill, a local fireman, arranged this picture on the fire-engine on the occasion of his wedding to Edith Cook of Wedmore in 1936. From left to right: Sam Durbin, Ted Isgar, Bill Isgar, Jim Filer, the bride, the bridegroom, Edward Cosh, Herbert Brooks, Ron Gray, and William Hill. The bridesmaid on the running-board is Rosemary Cook and alongside her is Reg Hill.

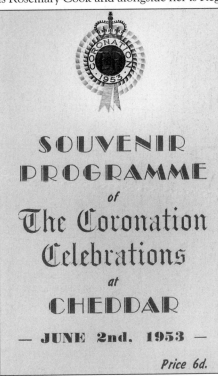

SOUVENIR
PROGRAMME
of
The Coronation
Celebrations
at
CHEDDAR
— JUNE 2nd, 1953 —

Price 6d.

Cheddar celebrated the coronation of Queen Elizabeth II with a grand programme of events which included: '9.40: United Thanksgiving Service at the Parish Church, 2.15: Carnival Judging, 3.15: Carnival Procession, 4.00: Picnic Tea for Children, 5.15: Short Concert by the Cheddar W.I. Choir, 5.30: Novelty Sports, 7.00: Country and Morris Dancing, 7.25: Display by Cheddar St John Ambulance Brigade, 7.40: Display by Cheddar Fire Brigade, 7.55: Pageant Play at the Vicarage 'They made the Royal Arms', 9.00: Dance at the Marquee at Froglands.'

The opening of Church House in 1895. In the procession from St Andrew's Church are the Bishop of Bath and Wells, the Very Rev J. Blake, and churchwardens J. Wookey and J. Coleman. One of the choirboys is Percy Raines. Close to the church gates can also be seen the bearded figure of Richard Cox Gough. There was a previous 'Church House' in the 16th and 17th centuries on the Wells side of the church at what is now Church Farm.

Seven

Sport and Leisure

Cheddar has for many years catered for the needs of its inhabitants by the formation of numerous clubs for both sport and leisure. Some have been long-standing, others came and went. The village is well blessed with sports facilities today, including those at Sharpham Road (with plans to improve these still further), the football ground on the Draycott Road, and the excellent leisure centre on the Kings of Wessex School Campus. However, it is interesting to look into the origin of some clubs in the village. For instance, Cheddar Lawn Tennis Club was formed in March 1924 and was indeed a 'lawn' tennis club. Their two courts were marked out on a field at Barrows Road and the grass was kept short in winter by grazing sheep! During the Second World War, membership dwindled to a mere 18 and the club only survived by holding numerous whist drives and the occasional dance to boost coffers. In 1957 the clubhouse was built and in the early 1980s all-weather courts were laid and floodlights provided. Apparently, the lease at Barrows Road is coming to an end and the future there is uncertain. The club, however, had the foresight to provide additional courts at Sharpham Road and so its history is likely to continue well beyond the current 73 years.

A tennis party, *c.* 1898. The third lady from the right standing is Mrs Emma Lewis. In the back row, on the left with the top hat, is Dr George Dale (the first chairman of Cheddar Parish Council in 1895) and, on the right, Gerald Hopkins's father.

Cheddar cricket team, 1899. From left to right, back row: R. Shore, A.D. Lewis, W. Harvey, G.R. Flower, Rev Lambrick, Mr Hussey (hon. secretary), G. Tyley, B. Gould; front row: W. Hills (groundsman), H. Bessant, E. Hopkins, T. King (captain), W. Bishop, T. Humphries, E. Mather, L. Hooper (treasurer). Although there is evidence of cricket being played in the Cheddar Valley before 1880 and a number of short-lived attempts to organise a club were made, it is only from 1882 that a cricket club emerged as a permanent feature in Cheddar life. Bert Gould recalls his grandfather playing for the club in 1885 and his father being involved with John Evans, Keith Pavey, Les Hewlett, and others, in restarting the club after the Second World War. They played at Yeodens then, on what is now the Kings of Wessex cricket pitch, with water for the wicket being carried in milk churns from the nearby river Yeo. In the mid-1950s the club moved to Bowdens Park, the home of Cheddar Football Club on the Draycott Road. 1964 saw the move to Sharpham Road, where they still play.

One of the first matches at Sharpham Road cricket ground was against a Somerset County Cricket Club team c. 1964. Seen here, with bats, are David Say (left) and George Williams (right) of Cheddar Cricket Club. To George Williams's right is Bill Alley, an Australian, who at that time was playing for Somerset. He was later to become a well-known umpire.

Cheddar Rugby Club in 1897, pictured close to the railway embankment. Among the players are Dr Openshaw (second left) and Messrs Chard, Bessant, Pavey, West, and Humphries. Cheddar Valley Rugby Club was formed around 1895. In the 1920s they played their matches on land near Wideatts Road. The club had a new lease of life in the early 1960s when they reformed and started playing on land at Sharpham Road alongside the reservoir. They now field as many as three teams and run a mini-rugby festival every year attracting both local teams and some from the surrounding counties.

Cheddar FC, 1936-37. The cup winners were, from left to right, back row: Gordon Lukins, Albert Dally, Teddy Binning, Jim Small, George Tozer; middle row: Jim Filer, Gordon Beagle, Bill Filer; front row: Reg Pavey, Reg Brown, Roy Adams, Will Adams, Les Scamp. The fixtures for the club were always displayed on a notice board in Bath Street between Channon's shop and W.S. Leigh's fruit shop (now Deane's). Cheddar Football Club was formed in 1892 and played on the cricket ground near the railway station. They moved to Lewis's ground, now the Kings of Wessex playing field, in 1926, and, later, to Ham Field, off Silver Street, where they played until 1950. Since then their home has been Bowdens Park on the Draycott Road.

A table-tennis club was formed by Norman Heal and others just before the Second World War, and continued until the early 1950s. The wallflowers seated at a club dance at the Cliff Hotel are from left to right: Cliff Radford, Terry King, Robert King, Nancy Ford, Amy Ford, Pat Askham, Fred Villis, Gloria Villis, Marjorie Foot (later Reed), and Chris Reed.

A gymkhana horse show, combined with the annual flower show, was a popular event in the village after the Second World War and was usually held at Froglands. Spectators in this picture from the early 1950s are: Charlie Stark (second from the left with the stick), Jack Hudson (third from the left), and, on the far right, Charlie Maunders, the founder of Maunders the builders in Barrows Road.

Cheddar swimming pool in Redcliffe Street was built in 1936 by John Little, a local builder, who had acquired the land from Mrs Statham, the owner of Cheddar Hall. Water was pumped directly from the nearby river Yeo and was filtered but not heated. The pool was eventually bought by the district council and was a very popular feature of the village for many years until it was demolished in 1996 to make way for a housing development.

Villagers pictured here at a Gay Nineties Club dinner in the 1950s at the Alexandra hall of the Cliff Hotel include Phyllis Ford, George Tiddy, Ted and Dot Heal, Nancy Tame, Natalie Brice, and Ann Card. This club was formed just after the Second World War by members interested in the type of dancing popular in the 1890s. Meetings were held in an upstairs room at the back of the Valley Hotel in Union Street, near the present-day library. Founder members were Nina White, Eveline Durston, and Reg Gould. The group later moved to Church House where they frequently held barn dances, some of which were broadcast on BBC radio. The group disbanded in the late 1950s.

There has been a Women's Institute in Cheddar since 1949. For many years WI members took part in an annual Christmas pantomime. In December 1969 at Church House it was *Dick Whittington and his Cat*, produced by Peggy Scourse and written by Eve Mills. They both appear in the centre of this picture with most of the cast and their helpers. Among those pictured are: Iris Crane, Rene Gray, Eileen Field, Margery Edwards, Gwen Chew, Margaret Barron, Pat Gardner, Joan Miles, Eileen Pople, Doreen Treasure, Muriel Gill, Ann Sparke, Marion Burnell, Marion Rooney, Joy Cross, Molly Tyson, Enid Greenow, June Ferris, Ethel Day, Nina White, Pat Senior, Dorothy Evans, Millie Brooks, Pearl Young, Jo Appleton, David Treasure, and Nan Reeves. The children at the front include Suzette Sparke, Dorothy Pople, Elizabeth Lane, Alison Brooks, Caroline Gardner, Joanne Gardner, Pauline Gray, Sandra Lane, Jennifer Sparke, Sarah Brooks, Ruth Treasure, Trevor Butcher, James Scourse, Andrew Yeates.

Eight
Wartime

While there is no wish to glorify war, these pictures could not be left out because they show something of the military connections of Cheddar both during and before both World Wars. Cheddar has been a place which the services have found useful both to accommodate their men during war and also for annual camps and exercises during peacetime.

Cheddar's war memorial stands at the junction of The Hayes, Station Road, and Wideatts Road, and is a well-looked-after area of the village always with an excellent display of flowers to show that the great sacrifice the men of the village made during the two World Wars is not forgotten. The memorial which was built in 1922 lists 34 men who lost their lives in the First World War and a further 12 who died during the Second World War. The wall at the right-hand side of this picture taken in the 1920s still exists although it may be a little lower. The trees on the left are in an area formerly known as Burnell's Orchard, on the corner where the Cheddar Tool Hire shop now stands.

The Royal Gloucestershire Hussars Imperial Yeomanry assembling following a service in St Andrew's Church, 1904.

In the early years of this century the Royal Gloucestershire Hussars Imperial Yeomanry visited Cheddar regularly for an annual camp in the Barrows Croft area. While at their camp, use was made of the firing range at Yoxter for rifle practice. This was reached by way of the Gorge where this picture was taken in 1904. It must have been a grand sight to see them riding past all the tourist attractions and, of course, their band would attract onlookers as military bands still do.

Cheddar Home Guard pictured at the old concrete works in Redcliffe Street during the Second World War. From left to right, back row: E. Packer, J. Pearce, J. Difford, -?-, R. Brice, R. Dyke, T. Evans, L. Winter, R. Lewis, E. Cosh, A. Pitman, middle row: -?-, R. Evans, H. Howard, T. Hill, -?-, C. Gregory, G. Gilling, A. Gough, A. Varney; front row: W. Baker, Mr George, G. Mansfield, W. Barber, C. Lewis, G.B. Brown, B. Butcher, S. Chick, J. Foot, M. Evans, C. Farthing, R. Thatcher.

502 Company of the Girls Training Corps parading in Cheddar in 1943. Terry King and Joyce Morris can be seen marching past the cinema. The purpose of the Girls Training Corps was to prepare girls aged 15 to 19 to be nurses and technicians prior to enlistment in the armed forces. In Cheddar they met at Church House.

The VE-day parade in May 1945 with the Red Cross and others parading along Bath Street.

The 1944 Remembrance Day parade outside what was then Lane's shop at the corner of Lower North Street and Station Road. The premises are now occupied by an estate agent. Several enemy aircraft were brought down in the vicinity of Cheddar during the Second World War. There was an RAF contingent which manned a decoy site on Blackdown – the area was lit up during air-raids to mislead German air-crew into thinking they were bombing Bristol. Many of the RAF personnel were billeted in Cheddar and, after the war, some married local girls and settled in the village, including Robert King, Bill Jones, Jim Morris, Mike Beddoes, and Harold Oakley.

Cheddar Civil Defence (Wardens Service), 1939-45. From left to right, back row: H. Hatch, H. Fraser, A. Pavey, R. Chinn, C. Heal, W. Ryall, W. Evans, R. Fowler, H. Strickland; third row; E. Dine, J. Cram, W. Eddy, E. Small, B. Jones, -?-, D. Gough, G. Simmons; second row: S. Ford, Mrs J. Tyson, C. Franklin, J. Tyson (head warden), Mrs J. Cram, G.K. Weaver, S. Bastard, J. Williams; front row: W. Hill, H. Tyson, R. Ford, J. Waterhouse, I. Wood.

J.H. Schroeder, on the right of this picture, was a Swiss banker who lived in the area. In the centre is Stanley Travis and on the left is Mr F.C. Tiarks, formerly of Webbington House. They are shown during the Second World War standing in a field of corn grown at Callow, bemoaning the lack of equipment to harvest the corn. The story is that Mr Tiarks wrote out a cheque for the necessary amount and the mechanical plant shown in the picture below was purchased with this money.

Nine

The Gorge

Cheddar Gorge has always been a place for people to come and stare in awe at the wonders of nature in the shape of huge cliffs and caves. The earliest recorded visit is by Henry, archdeacon of Huntingdon, in 1130. Daniel Defoe was a visitor in 1720, and Collinson the well-known historian visited in 1791. However, it was not until the 19th century that development of the area as the tourist attraction recognisable today began.

In 1837, George Cox, who worked a mill on the site of the Gorge (Cliff) Hotel, stumbled on what is now Cox's cave while trying to make room to expand his business. He quickly saw the commercial potential and soon was showing visitors around the cave and providing dinners and teas in the gardens of the Cliff Hotel. In 1870, Richard Cox Gough, a cousin of the Cox family, came to Cheddar, acquired the lease of a cave in 1873 and about 1890 discovered the present Gough's showcave. In 1902 a 9,000-year-old male skeleton was discovered in the cave. Recent DNA tests have shown a close association between this man and a contemporary school-teacher in the village.

The railway came to Cheddar in 1869 and heralded an era of mass tourism. The need to entertain this large number of tourists was seen by Rowland Pavey who built a 'Temperance Hotel' by the foot of Jacob's Ladder.

Some of these cottages still exist in the Gorge although they have mostly been converted into shops and tea-rooms. Sycamore House, on the right, stood on what is now the site of the tourist information office.

Tommy Carr's cottage was situated in the Gorge and is pictured here on a postcard sent in 1907. The cottage is said to have originated as a 'sundowner' cottage. There was an old law which allowed a person to put up a cottage on the side of the road providing that it was built and had smoke coming out of the chimney by sundown. The cottage was demolished when road improvements were carried out in the 1920s. Richard Cox Gough's smoking house, the small circular building in the centre of the picture, was built as a haven for his smoking. It was demolished some time after he died.

The waterfall by the Gorge Hotel (formerly the Cliff Hotel) is a feature in the Gorge. The pool above it was originally the header pool for the mill situated on the site. Some of the buildings shown on the left of the picture no longer exist and the waterfall is somewhat narrower since the extension to the hotel was built.

Dag Hole by the White Hart public house is a popular area for tourists today. It has lost some of the rustic charm shown here but the cottages are still there even if some are now shops.

THE GARDENS, CLIFF HOTEL, CHEDDAR   S 545

The tea-gardens associated with the Cliff Hotel were a very popular place for visitors to refresh themselves on hot summer days, no doubt with strawberries, when in season, and cream. This card is postmarked August 1937 although we know the picture predates that. The area shown is probably where the crazy-golf is now found.

The Lion Rock Hotel is still in the Gorge today. It has strong associations with Richard Cox Gough, the founder of Gough's Cave. In fact it is thought that he lived there at one time when it was called Lion Rock House.

There was a bad landslip and rockfall in the Gorge on 4 February 1906. After this, quarrying ceased and the Lion Rock side of the Gorge was purchased by the National Trust following a countrywide appeal. This card is postmarked 22 February 1906.

In September 1959, 22-year-old Rudolf Omankowsky walked a tight-rope across Cheddar Gorge. Huge crowds gathered below to witness the occasion. A new wire rope had to be purchased from Bristol to span the width of the Gorge and it was not until he was on the wire that Omankowsky realised the rope was heavily greased and was causing him to slip. He paused several times in his crossing to wipe off the grease and at one stage he sat on the wire and removed a pair of his thick socks and used them to remove the grease from both his shoes and the rope. Two other members of the team, Rudi's brother and his wife, experienced similar problems when they drove their tyreless motor-cycle on the wire as the grease made the wheels spin. Omankowsky later presided at the Centre Nationale des Arts du Cirque, at Chalon sur Marne in France.

Jacob's Ladder and Pavey's Tower c. 1910. The original Pavey's Tower was built about 1908 by Rowland Pavey who was anxious to cash in on the tourist boom in the Gorge generated by Cox and Gough. Pavey had searched in vain for a cave which he could open to tourists and he even constructed one but it was never a success and ended up being the exit to the neighbouring Cox's cave. Later, Pavey decided to build the 274 steps of Jacob's Ladder in order to take the tourists up to enjoy the views from his observation tower above the Gorge. Adjacent to the tower was 'Joyland', a pleasure ground created by Pavey, with a shooting gallery, several cable runways, and a restaurant to which the food was sent up on a 'dumb-waiter' cable arrangement in straw-lined boxes to keep it warm. At the foot of Jacob's Ladder was Pavey's Temperance Hotel, described as 'nestling at the foot of the Cheddar Cliffs'. The original Pavey's Tower was destroyed by a storm in 1930 and was later rebuilt in steel to an improved design. The present tower has gone through several modifications but it still presents a wonderful viewpoint over the surrounding area.

The aerial runway, one of the attractions at Pavey's Hill Pleasure Grounds (or 'Joyland' as it was also known), *c.* 1910.

The Cliff Hotel has been a very popular place since the early part of this century, both for tourists to stay and for local people to meet. It was built on the site of Cox's corn-mill. At the rear of the hotel near the waterfall there was a large garden (*see page 87*), where the ever-popular cream teas were served. The hotel was a regular meeting place for the 'Cyclists Touring Club'; indeed, until not long ago, their logo was mounted on the outside wall. In recent years it has been renamed 'The Cheddar Gorge Hotel'.

Sycamore House, opposite Derrick's Tea Rooms, *c*. 1907. 'Furnished Apartments' were advertised here 'with accommodation for cyclists and motorists. Luncheons and Teas at moderate charges. Parties catered for'. Specialities were 'Cave Tea Room Fruit Salads and Cream'. The house was described as 'picturesquely situated, facing the far famed Lion Rock and immediately between the two famous caves'. Sycamore House was pulled down in 1959 after being damaged by a rock fall. The tourist information office now stands on the site.

Pavey's Temperance Hotel at the foot of Jacob's Ladder. Only the rear part of the building survives today, as Old Rowland's Gift Shop. The remainder was demolished for road widening.

Derrick's Tea Rooms is probably one of the oldest established businesses in the Gorge. This picture shows it *c.* 1925. The advertisement on the front of the building is for William Small's 'Genuine Cheddar Cheese Depot'. The boy in the picture is the late Ron Derrick. His mother Alice started the business and Ron's widow Marjorie only recently sold the tea-rooms after running them for over forty years.

Weeks Tea Gardens, *c.* 1910. These were where the Edinburgh Woollen Mill shop and adjacent car park are now located at the bottom of the Gorge. Ernest Weeks, on the right, was a competitive cyclist, winning a total of 29 cups and medals. The other cyclist on the left is thought to be Walter Pym. The old shirt factory and The Bays pond can be seen in the background.

The cave guides were an important part of the tourist industry and were mostly local people. Some of those pictured here c. 1900 are, from left to right: Reg Athay, Arthur Hicks, Fred Bessant, Stewart Norton, George Heal, PC Benjafield (who helped out at times), Vic Painter, and Vic Herring. Vic Painter was for many years head guide and worked with the Gough family in the exploration of the caves.

There was a large staff employed at Gough's Cave to cater for the needs of visitors. This picture is thought to have been taken about 1934. The manager of the showcave then was a Mr Vanstone and among the 94 members of staff shown are: Jack Sampson, Mr Sargent, George Nicholson, Mrs Hart, and Audrey Bishop (all in the back row); others include: George Welchman, Bill Dean, Reg Hembury, Percy Channon, Harold Chinn, Don Herring, Miss Cox, Mrs Cox, George Heal, Miss Robins, and John Cox.

Before the First World War visitors to the Gorge were often carried from the railway station to the Gorge by a horse-drawn vehicle, here seen outside the Cliff Hotel. The driver is John Coles and the carriage's name was *The Pride of The Valley*, seen boldly displayed on the side.

Charabanc trips to Cheddar were very popular. Visitors would have their photograph taken outside the caves before entering and the pictures would be available for them when they came out. The young hatless couple in the middle of this coach is Elizabeth Jane Nicholson (*née* Hendy) and Francis Graham Nicholson, who were on honeymoon from London in 1924. By the strangest of coincidences their son Graham is a member of Cheddar Valley U3A (the authors of this book) and lives in Shipham.

William and Arthur Gough, sons of Richard Cox Gough, have joined this 1920s picture with their visitors. They can be seen on the extreme left and right of the picture.

The modern entrance to Gough's Cave, together with the 'Cave Man Restaurant', *c.* 1950. The building was designed by Sir Geoffrey Jellicoe and was completed in 1934 by Stones of Bristol. It was one of the country's first all-concrete structures and won a design award. An unusual feature was a glass-bottomed fish-pool in the roof which could be viewed from either above or below. The pool was eventually filled in during the 1980s but the glass blocks are still there. The previous entrance to the caves was at a higher level with steps to climb. The new entrance at road level was made in the 1960s.